Katrin Cargill's

simple curtains

creative ideas & 20 step-by-step projects

Katrin Cargill's
simple curtains

creative ideas & 20 step-by-step projects

Katrin Cargill

photography by **James Merrell**

RYLAND
PETERS
& SMALL

LONDON NEW YORK

For this edition:
Designers Saskia Janssen and
    Sarah Fraser
Editor Miriam Hyslop
Production Sheila Smith
Art Director Gabriella Le Grazie
Publishing Director Alison Starling
Illustrator Michael Hill

Library of Congress Cataloging-in-Publication Data

Cargill, Katrin.
  Katrin Cargill's simple curtains : creative ideas &
20 step-by-step
projects / Katrin Cargill ; photography by James
Merrell.-- 2nd ed.
    p. cm.
  Includes bibliographical references and index.
  ISBN 1-84172-794-6 (alk. paper)
  1. Draperies. I. Title: Simple curtains. II. Title.
TT390.C27 2005
646.2'1--dc22   2004025140

First published in the United States in
1998 and reissued with amendments in
2005 by Ryland Peters & Small
519 Broadway
5th Floor
New York NY 10012
www.rylandpeters.com

Text © Katrin Cargill 1998, 2005
Design and photographs © Ryland
Peters & Small 1998, 2005

Printed in China.

Contents

In recent years there has been a revolution in the world of curtains. Grandeur and formality have been replaced with simplicity and freshness—enormous swags and tails made from acres of brocade, ornate valances, and flouncy balloon shades have given way to clean lines, subtle textures, and strong colors. This impetus toward a mood of effortless elegance has resulted in a new freedom when it comes to making curtains. Simple curtains make stylish statements that are subtly effective rather than overly dramatic. They will enliven and enhance any window without dominating it, and because they do not require yards and yards of material, you can use that irresistible fabric without breaking the bank and blowing half your decorating budget.

For this book, I have searched out simple curtain ideas that are practical, uncomplicated, and well-suited to the windows they have been made for. So often, one sees a terrific pair of curtains on completely the wrong window. Try to be sensitive to the dimensions of the window and the proportions of the room. There are fewer rules than ever before for lengths and widths of curtains, so I have tried to show as many examples as possible of treatments that work because they are sensitive to scale. I hope that this book will inspire you to realize the potential of your own windows!

Katrin Cargill

use of fabrics

Fabric comes in a wide and dazzling array of colors, textures, and patterns. By piecing together fabric in unexpected combinations, you will achieve innovative and original effects. Be bold, and experiment with different textures and different designs, all cunningly combined in a single pair of curtains. Creative use of fabrics will allow you to make elegant, stylish, and totally unique window treatments.

below *An inexpensive slubby cotton has been lined and interlined for a luxurious and opulent effect. The bobbled border at the top of the curtains creates textural interest.*
below left *Black and white antique toile de Jouy curtains are teamed with an irreverent red bobble fringing to create a timeless look at an elegant window. Unexpected combinations like this will enliven a simple pair of curtains.*

left *A stylish alternative to the ubiquitous white nets. A checked red and white voile serves the same purpose—privacy—but with a little more verve and color.*

below left to right *Ready-made tab-topped curtains are dyed in oranges, yellows, and reds. The fabric filters light and creates a dappled effect. Two pairs of curtains on separate poles, one made from flimsy voile and the other cotton moiré, create an interesting layered look. The narrow edging on these pretty toile de Jouy curtains brings definition to the leading edge and frames an unusual round window; an upholstered slipper chair has been covered in the same fabric and continues the feminine yet unfussy theme. Crisp white cotton allows light to filter into a room, yet provides both privacy and shade.*

yellow checks

These cheerful, colorful yellow curtains are guaranteed to bring a relaxed, sunny atmosphere to any room, even in the darkest depths of winter. They are made of three different panels of coordinating fabrics joined horizontally; vivid scarlet braid is sewn on the front of the curtain over the seams to conceal them. The bold checks and braid have a pleasing rustic simplicity that is echoed by the simple ties that hold the curtains to an iron pole.

materials & equipment

three different main fabrics

lining fabric

5/8-inch (1.5 cm) wide red braid

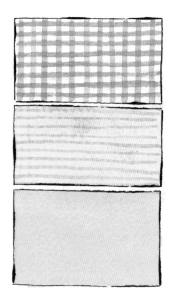

1 Measure the window to calculate fabric quantities (see Techniques, page 96). Each panel occupies one third of the drop of the finished curtain. Add ⅝ inch (1.5 cm) to the length of each panel for each seam. Add another 3 inches (8 cm) to the top panel for the heading and 6½ inches (16 cm) to the bottom panel for the hem. Each curtain must be the width of the pole plus a 4¾-inch (12 cm) hem allowance. The lining fabric must be 1¾ inches (4 cm) smaller than the finished curtain all around. Cut out the fabric.

2 Place the top panel on a flat surface with the middle panel on top, right sides together and raw edges aligned. Pin, baste, and machine stitch the two panels together, using a ⅝ inch (1.5 cm) seam allowance and matching the checks as best you can. Press open the seam. Attach the bottom panel to the middle panel in the same way.

3 Cut two strips of braid to the width of the curtain. Center the braid over the seams between the panels on the right side of the curtain. Pin, baste, and machine stitch down both edges of the braid.

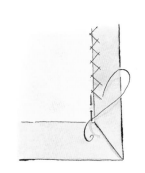

4 Press in a 2½-inch (6 cm) hem at each side of the curtain and a double 3-inch (8 cm) hem at the bottom. Press in the angled miters (see Techniques, page 100). Pin and baste the hems in place. Herringbone stitch the side hems. Slipstitch the bottom hem and the miters.

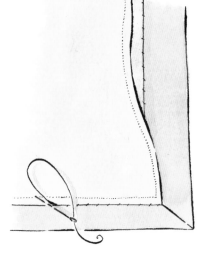

5 Cut out the lining. Press in a ¾-inch (2 cm) hem along each side edge and a double ¾-inch (2 cm) hem along the bottom. Pin and baste the hems. Miter the corners (see Techniques, page 100) and machine stitch the hems in place.

6 Place the curtain on a flat surface, wrong side up. Place the lining on top, right side up. Match the corners of the lining with the mitered corners of the curtain and align the top raw edges. Pin the curtain and lining together along the top raw edges. Pin and baste the lining to the curtain. Slip stitch the lining to the curtain fabric. Leave the bottom of the lining open to make the curtain hang better.

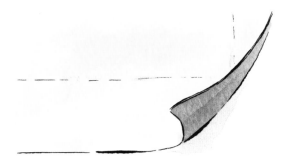

6 At each side of the drape, press in a 2½-inch (6 cm) fold over the interlining. Then fold up a 3-inch (8 cm) hem at the bottom edge and press in place. Fold in and press the angled miters (see Techniques, page 100) at the bottom corners of the drape.

7 Pin and baste the hems in place. Herringbone stitch the side and bottom hems and slipstitch the miters.

8 Place the lining right side down on a flat surface. Press a ¾-inch (2 cm) fold down each side edge of the lining and a double ¾-inch (2 cm) hem along the bottom edge. Miter the corners and press. Pin, baste, and machine stitch the side and bottom hems in place.

9 Place the drape on a flat surface, interlined side up. Place the lining on top, right side up. Match the corners of the lining with the mitered corners of the main fabric and align the top raw edges. Pin the drape and lining together along their top edges, making sure the material lies completely flat. Baste, then slipstitch the edges of the lining to the drape. Leaving the bottom of the lining open will make the drape hang better.

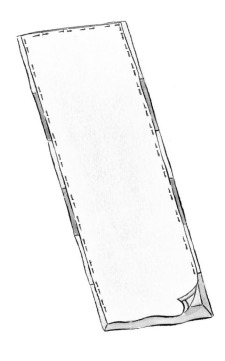

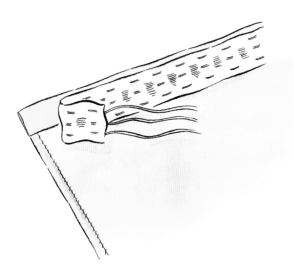

10 Cut the heading tape to the width of the curtain plus 1¼ inches (3 cm) at each end. Knot the strings at the leading edge and leave them loose at the other. At the top of the curtain press a 3-inch (8 cm) fold to the wrong side. Pin the tape over the fold, ½ inch (1 cm) below the edge, tucking in the raw ends. Pin, baste, and machine stitch the tape in place. Pull the strings and knot the end. Insert the hooks and hang the curtain.

two-way stripes

The beauty of delicate sheers is that they can diffuse bright sunshine or conceal an unattractive view without obscuring natural light. Here, in a simple arrangement requiring little sewing, striped voile curtains are suspended from metal eyelets punched through the fabric and hung from hooks screwed above the window. The curtains can either hang loose or be knotted out of the way. A chic contrasting heading strip is formed by turning the stripes to run horizontally across the top.

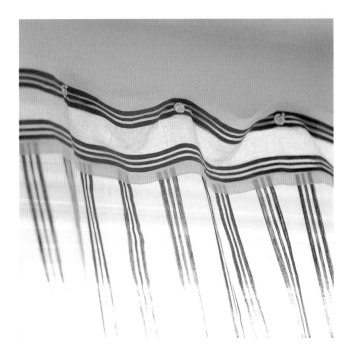

materials & equipment

striped voile fabric

metal eyelets

hole-punch kit

hooks

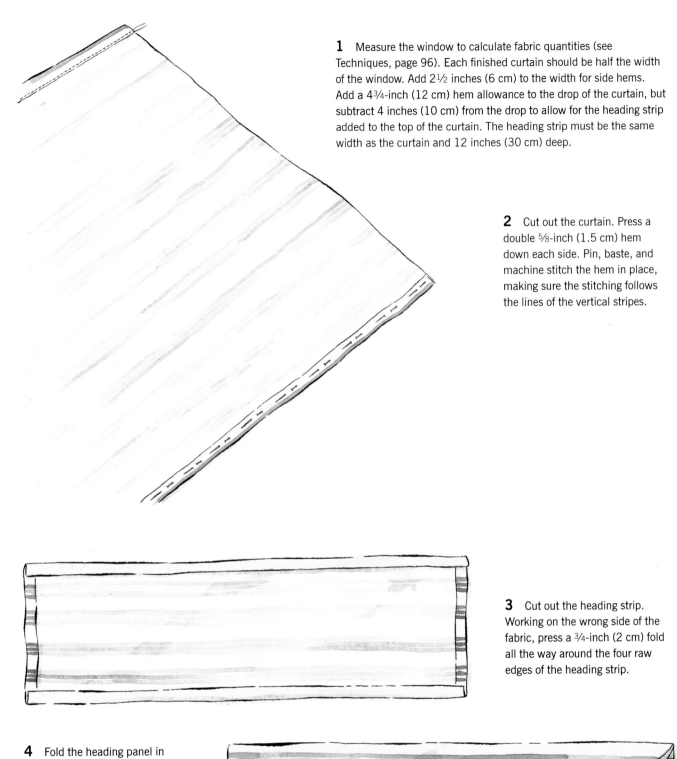

1   Measure the window to calculate fabric quantities (see Techniques, page 96). Each finished curtain should be half the width of the window. Add 2½ inches (6 cm) to the width for side hems. Add a 4¾-inch (12 cm) hem allowance to the drop of the curtain, but subtract 4 inches (10 cm) from the drop to allow for the heading strip added to the top of the curtain. The heading strip must be the same width as the curtain and 12 inches (30 cm) deep.

2   Cut out the curtain. Press a double ⅝-inch (1.5 cm) hem down each side. Pin, baste, and machine stitch the hem in place, making sure the stitching follows the lines of the vertical stripes.

3   Cut out the heading strip. Working on the wrong side of the fabric, press a ¾-inch (2 cm) fold all the way around the four raw edges of the heading strip.

4   Fold the heading panel in half across the width, wrong sides together, making sure that the folded edges meet. Press along the fold.

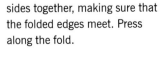

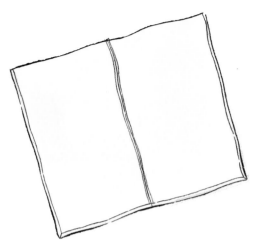

6 The lining should be 1¾ inches (4 cm) smaller all around than the finished drape. Cut out the lining fabric and join widths if necessary (see Techniques, page 98). To finish the edges turn, and press a ¾-inch (2 cm) hem along each side edge of the lining and a double ¾-inch (2 cm) hem along the bottom edge. Miter the corners and press. Pin, baste, and machine stitch the side and bottom hems in place.

7 Place the drape on a flat surface, wrong side up. Place the lining on top of the drape, right side up. Match the corners of the lining to the mitered corners of the main fabric and align the top raw edges. There should be a border of drape fabric showing all around the lining. Pin the drape and lining together along their top raw edges. Pin, baste, and slipstitch the folded edges of the lining to the drape. Leave the bottom of the lining open to make the drape hang better.

8 Cut the pencil-pleat heading tape to the width of the drape plus an additional 1¼ inches (3 cm) at each end. Knot the strings at the leading edge and leave them loose at the other.

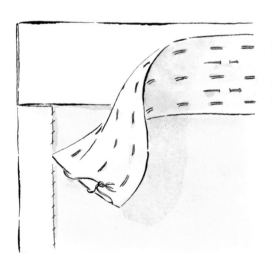

9 At the top raw edge of the drape, turn down a 3-inch (8 cm) fold to the wrong side. Press in place. Position the heading tape along the top of the drape, ½ inch (1 cm) below the folded top edge. Tuck under the raw ends of the tape and the knotted strings at the leading edge. The turnover will be concealed by the heading tape. Pin, baste, and machine stitch around the edges of the heading tape through all the layers of fabric.

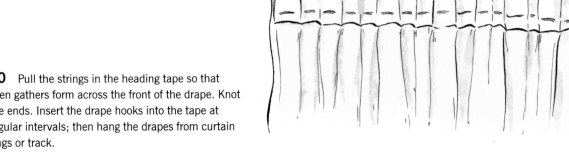

10 Pull the strings in the heading tape so that even gathers form across the front of the drape. Knot the ends. Insert the drape hooks into the tape at regular intervals; then hang the drapes from curtain rings or track.

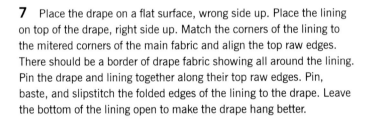

headings

A curtain is attached to a track, rod, or pole by the heading—the decorative top of the curtain. From formal pleated headings hung from antique poles with elaborate gilt finials to informal ties loosely knotted around an iron rod, a heading sets the mood for the curtains. A wide variety of heading tapes is now available, so creating pinch pleats, goblet pleats, soft gathers, and many other heading styles is now easier and more achievable than ever before.

A variety of headings:
far left *Red-checked voile with a cased heading for a softly gathered effect.*
left *Pinch pleats create an elegant, formal feel.*
below left *Gathering tape gives a gently ruffled heading.*

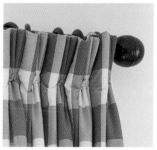

below far left *A tightly gathered pencil pleat heading gives a ruched effect that adds interest to plain cream curtains.*
below center *A simple heading with rings attached to hooks.*
below right *Unusual double curtains are attached to a pair of poles by means of clip-on curtain rings, which require no sewing.*
bottom *A crisp check curtain with neatly knotted ties.*

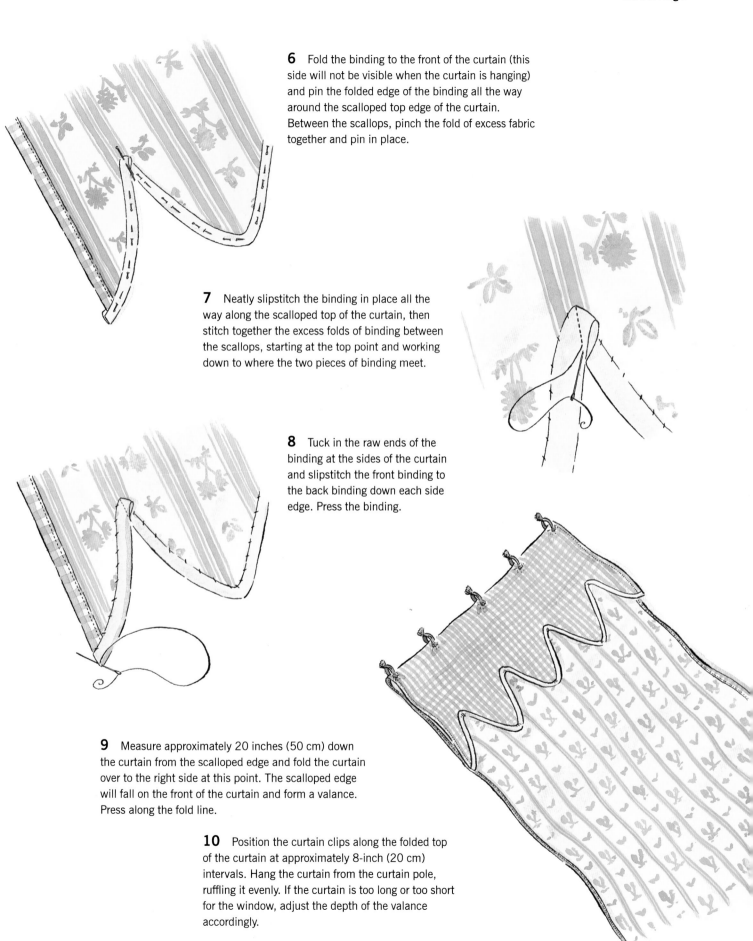

6 Fold the binding to the front of the curtain (this side will not be visible when the curtain is hanging) and pin the folded edge of the binding all the way around the scalloped top edge of the curtain. Between the scallops, pinch the fold of excess fabric together and pin in place.

7 Neatly slipstitch the binding in place all the way along the scalloped top of the curtain, then stitch together the excess folds of binding between the scallops, starting at the top point and working down to where the two pieces of binding meet.

8 Tuck in the raw ends of the binding at the sides of the curtain and slipstitch the front binding to the back binding down each side edge. Press the binding.

9 Measure approximately 20 inches (50 cm) down the curtain from the scalloped edge and fold the curtain over to the right side at this point. The scalloped edge will fall on the front of the curtain and form a valance. Press along the fold line.

10 Position the curtain clips along the folded top of the curtain at approximately 8-inch (20 cm) intervals. Hang the curtain from the curtain pole, ruffling it evenly. If the curtain is too long or too short for the window, adjust the depth of the valance accordingly.

button-on silk

A luxurious heavy swathe of raw silk hangs in a dramatic single sweep at a sash window, caught to one side by the squiggle of a minimal metal tieback. At the top of the curtain, tabs made from the same fabric are buttoned onto the top of the curtain, then hooked over small shell-shaped cupboard or drawer knobs. The fluid swags and folds of the fabric provide a classical flavor, but the unusual heading brings an unexpected modern twist to this simple arrangement.

materials & equipment

heavy raw silk

3—4 small, decorative drawer or cupboard knobs

6—8 silk-covered buttons

metal tieback

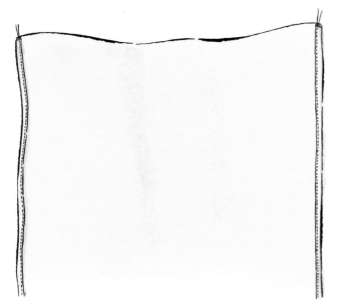

1 To calculate how much fabric is required, measure your window (see Techniques, page 96). The curtain must be the width of the window plus enough extra fabric to allow the curtain to swag between the knobs to which it is buttoned. Add an extra 10½ inches (26 cm) to the length for hem and heading and 5 inches (12 cm) to the width for side hems. Join widths if necessary (see Techniques, page 98).

2 Press a double 1¼-inch (3 cm) hem to the wrong side down each side of the curtain, and pin, baste, and machine stitch in place.

3 Press a double 2½-inch (6 cm) fold to the wrong side all the way across the top of the curtain. Pin, baste, and machine stitch this in place.

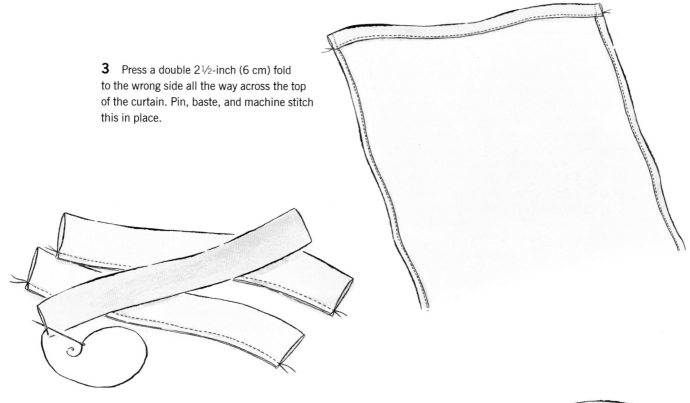

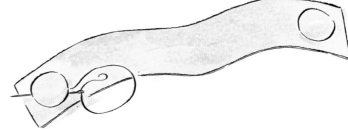

4 Decide how many knobs you are going to hang your curtain from (this will depend on the width of your window frame) and screw them to the wall or the top of the window frame at regular intervals. You will need one tab for each knob. Cut out a strip of silk 3 x 10½ inches (8 x 26 cm) for each tab. Make the tabs (see Techniques, page 101).

5 You will need two silk-covered buttons for each tab. Hand-stitch a button 1 inch (2.5 cm) in from each end of the tab.

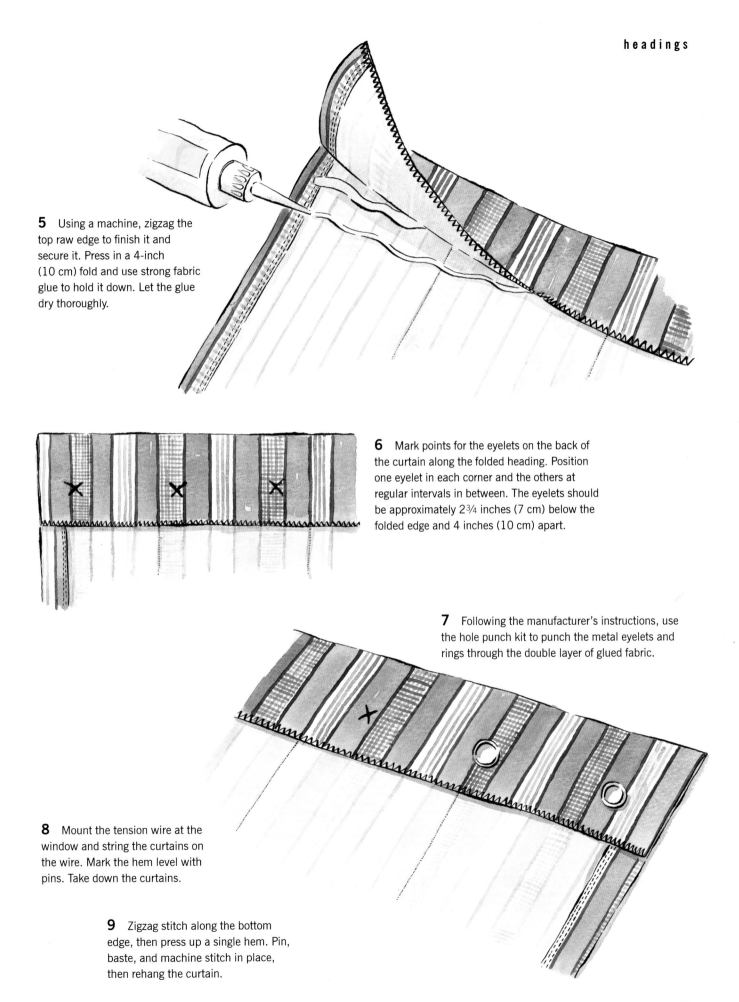

5 Using a machine, zigzag the top raw edge to finish it and secure it. Press in a 4-inch (10 cm) fold and use strong fabric glue to hold it down. Let the glue dry thoroughly.

6 Mark points for the eyelets on the back of the curtain along the folded heading. Position one eyelet in each corner and the others at regular intervals in between. The eyelets should be approximately 2¾ inches (7 cm) below the folded edge and 4 inches (10 cm) apart.

7 Following the manufacturer's instructions, use the hole punch kit to punch the metal eyelets and rings through the double layer of glued fabric.

8 Mount the tension wire at the window and string the curtains on the wire. Mark the hem level with pins. Take down the curtains.

9 Zigzag stitch along the bottom edge, then press up a single hem. Pin, baste, and machine stitch in place, then rehang the curtain.

tie-on sheers

These floaty unlined voile curtains hanging
at a French door create a light and airy effect.
The wrought-iron pole is attached not to the
window frame but to the ceiling, and the
length of the curtains and the generous swathes of
fabric emphasize rather than obscure the fine
proportions of the elegant glass doors.
The bobbly tassel fringe provides an interesting
textural contrast with the economical
outlines of the simple metal tieback.

materials & equipment

white voile

tassel fringe

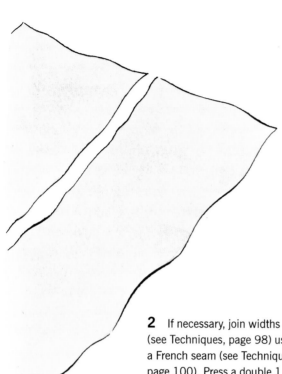

1   To calculate the amount of fabric required, measure the window (see Techniques, page 96). The width of each single curtain must be equal to the entire length of the pole to give enough fullness in the width. Add 4¾ inches (12 cm) to the width for side hems and 9 inches (22 cm) to the length for hem and heading. Cut out the fabric (see Techniques, page 98).

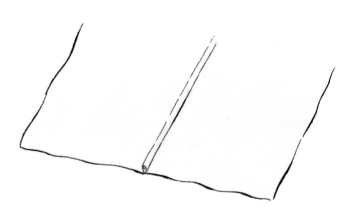

2   If necessary, join widths (see Techniques, page 98) using a French seam (see Techniques, page 100). Press a double 1¼-inch (3 cm) fold down both sides of the curtain, and pin, baste, and machine stitch in place.

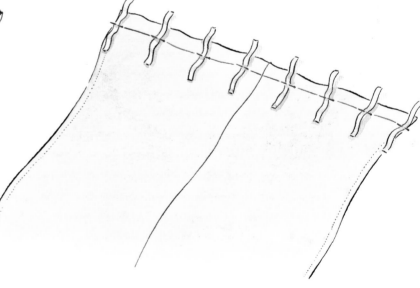

3   The number of ties needed will depend on the width of the curtain, but there should be one tie approximately every 6 inches (15 cm). Cut out strips of voile, each one 2 x 18 inches (5 x 45 cm), and make the ties for each curtain (see Techniques, page 101).

4   Place the curtain right side up on a flat surface, and mark a line across the curtain, 4¾ inches (12 cm) below the top raw edge. Position a tie at each top corner of the curtain and space the other ties evenly between them. Pin and baste the midpoint of each tie to the line, then machine stitch all the way along the marked line, securing the ties to the curtain.

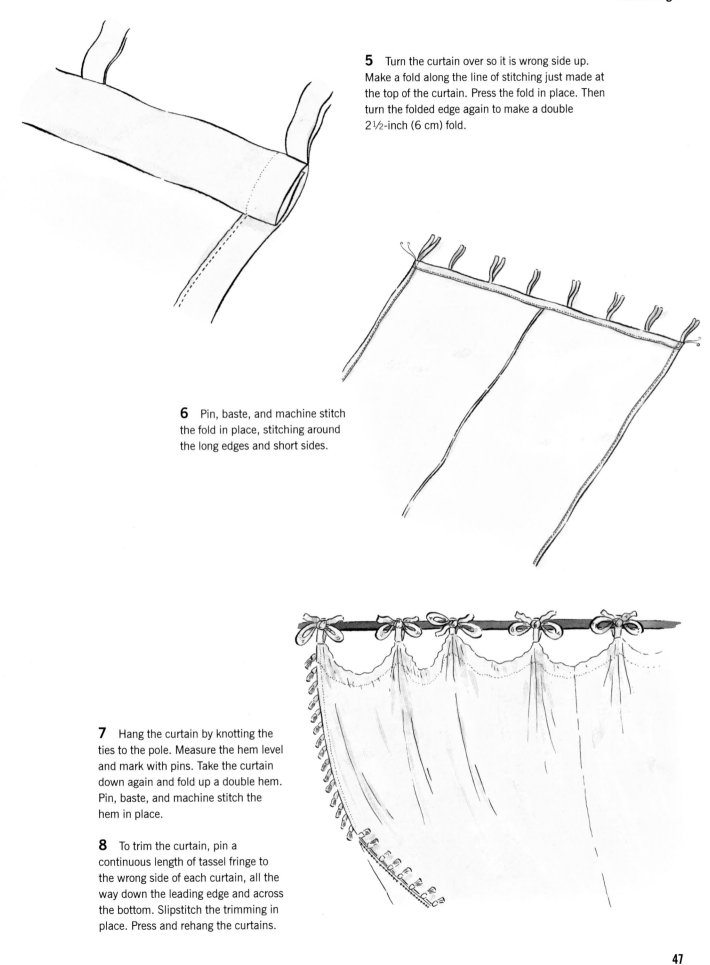

5 Turn the curtain over so it is wrong side up. Make a fold along the line of stitching just made at the top of the curtain. Press the fold in place. Then turn the folded edge again to make a double 2½-inch (6 cm) fold.

6 Pin, baste, and machine stitch the fold in place, stitching around the long edges and short sides.

7 Hang the curtain by knotting the ties to the pole. Measure the hem level and mark with pins. Take the curtain down again and fold up a double hem. Pin, baste, and machine stitch the hem in place.

8 To trim the curtain, pin a continuous length of tassel fringe to the wrong side of each curtain, all the way down the leading edge and across the bottom. Slipstitch the trimming in place. Press and rehang the curtains.

valances

Valances add a perfect finishing touch to an attractive window treatment and can be major decorative elements in their own right. Valances can be stiffened and shaped pieces of fabric hung from a board, or softer in effect and unstiffened. They can be used alone or teamed with matching or contrasting drapes.

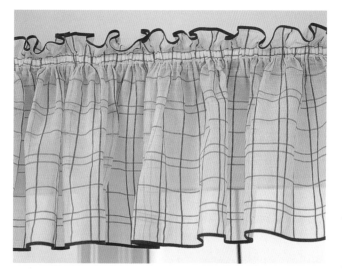

left *A checked voile valance is edged top and bottom with a thin red trim, which emphasizes the tight ruffles of the gathering tape heading. Valances are ideally suited to windows that do not need a full curtain.*

below left *This panel of fabric acts as a valance at a small kitchen window. Small-scale red-and-white gingham has a cased heading into which an expansion rod has been inserted. The fabric is held out of the way with thin ties. A quick and easy window treatment that need not be a permanent fixture.*

below *An unassuming pair of striped cotton curtains is made much more immposing by the addition of a classic shaped valance. Vertically striped curtains and valances can appear to lengthen the proportions of small, wide windows.*

8 Clip around the zigzags, so when you turn the valance right side out the zigzags will lie flat and not pucker.

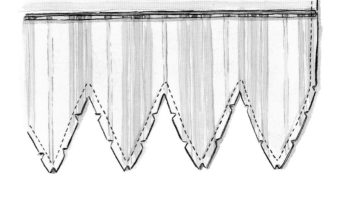

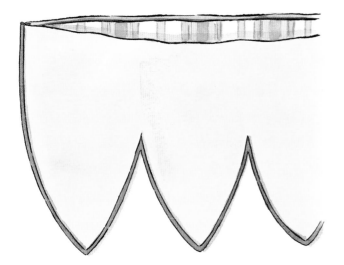

9 Turn the valance right side out. Push out the points of the zigzags with a knitting needle. Press a ⅝-inch (1.5 cm) fold to the inside all the way along both the open straight edges at the top of the valance.

10 Cut the heading tape to the width of the valance. Knot the threads at one end, but leave them loose at the other. Pin and baste the heading tape along the top edge of the back of the valance, making sure the top edge of the heading tape aligns with the folded top edges of the valance and tucking the raw ends of the tape under at both ends. Machine stitch all around the heading tape, close to the edges.

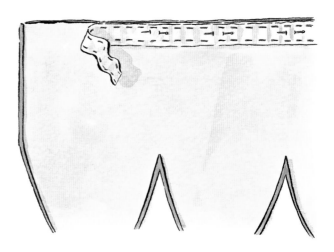

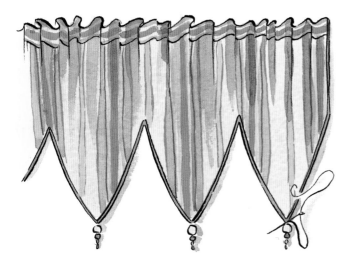

11 Pull the strings of the tape into a loose gather, and knot the end. Hand-sew two or three beads to the very tip of each zigzag for decoration.

12 Insert the curtain hooks at even intervals along the tape. Hang the valance from curtain rings on your pole.

red-trimmed voile

This simple yet stylish all-in-one single curtain and valance is ideally suited to French doors. The translucent voile allows sunlight to filter into the room, creating a warm glow of diffused light. The voluminous folds of the voile feel wonderfully lavish, while the vivid scarlet ribbon adds definition to the valance. If the door is frequently in use, a metal tieback mounted at the side of it would allow the curtain to be neatly caught to one side, out of the way.

materials & equipment

white voile fabric

1 3/4-inch (3 cm) wide silk binding

clip-on curtain rings

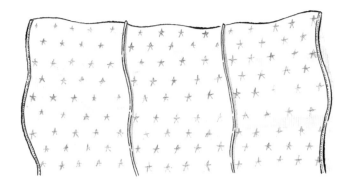

1 Measure the window to calculate fabric quantities (see Techniques, page 96). Add 2¾ inches (7 cm) to the length for the hem. The fabric must be three times the width of the pole plus 4¾ inches (12 cm) for side hems. Cut out the fabric. Join widths using a French seam (see Techniques, page 100). Pin, baste, and machine stitch a double 1¼-inch (3 cm) hem down each side of the curtain.

2 The valance should be one-sixth of the length of the finished curtain and the same width plus the same hem allowances. Cut out the fabric, then join widths as for the main curtain. Press a double 1¼-inch (3 cm) hem down each side. Pin, baste, and machine stitch in place.

3 Place the valance right side up on top of the right side of the main curtain, lining up the raw edges at the top. Pin, baste, and machine stitch together using a ½-inch (1 cm) seam allowance.

4 Make two strips of red silk binding (see Techniques, page 101). Each strip should be equal to the width of the curtain plus 1 inch (2.5 cm) for the end turnings. Turn and press ¼ inch (5 mm) to the wrong side all along the long edges of the binding. Fold and press the strips in half lengthwise so the folded edges meet.

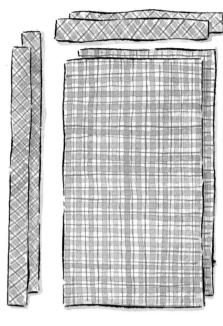

1 Calculate the size of your mounting board (see Techniques, page 98). It should be 3 inches (8 cm) deep. Cut it out and screw eyelets along the front and side edges at 3-inch (8 cm) intervals. Attach it to the wall.

2 Measure the window and the board to calculate how much fabric you will need (see Techniques, page 96). As the curtains have a loose pencil-pleat heading, the fabric must be at least twice the width of the board plus 3 inches (8 cm) for the side hems. Add 9½ inches (24 cm) to the length for heading and hem. The border requires two strips of fabric cut on the bias, both 8½ inches (22 cm) deep, one the same length as the curtain and the other the same length as the width of the curtain. The bow requires four strips of material, two measuring 12 x 24 inches (30 x 60 cm) and two 2 x 8 inches (5 x 20 cm). The lining is 1¾ inches (4 cm) smaller all around than the finished curtain.

3 Cut out the fabric for the curtains and border, joining widths if necessary (see Techniques, page 98). Place the border strips right sides together. At one end, pin and baste the strips together at a 45° angle, running down diagonally from the top corner. Check that the angle of the seam is correct and that the checks match, then machine stitch, stopping ¾ inch (2 cm) from the bottom of the strip. Open out the border and press a ¾-inch (2 cm) fold to the wrong side all around the inner edge.

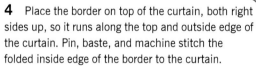

4 Place the border on top of the curtain, both right sides up, so it runs along the top and outside edge of the curtain. Pin, baste, and machine stitch the folded inside edge of the border to the curtain.

5 Turn the curtain over so it is right side down. Press a 1¾-inch (4 cm) hem along the sides and a 3-inch (8 cm) double hem at the bottom. Press in the angled miters (see Techniques, page 100). Pin and baste the hems. Herringbone stitch the side hems and slipstitch the base hem and the miters.

6 Cut out the lining, joining widths if necessary (see Techniques, page 98). Turn under and press a ¾-inch (2 cm) hem along the sides of the lining and a double ¾-inch (2 cm) hem along the bottom. Miter the corners. Pin, baste, and machine stitch the side and bottom hems in place.

7 Place the curtain right side down with the lining on top, right side up. Pin the curtain and lining together at the top. Pin, baste, and slipstitch the lining to the curtain at the sides. Leave the bottom of the lining open—it will help the curtain hang better.

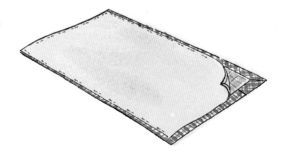

7 To make the deep pleat in the curtain, turn it over so it is lying right side down with the lining uppermost. Fold the leading edge of the curtain back on itself along the seam line where the toile de Jouy is joined to the main curtain fabric.

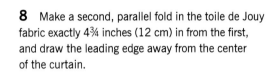

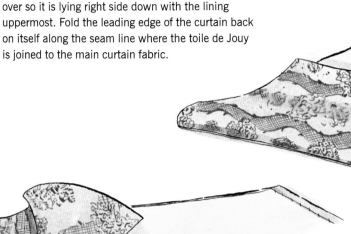

8 Make a second, parallel fold in the toile de Jouy fabric exactly 4¾ inches (12 cm) in from the first, and draw the leading edge away from the center of the curtain.

9 Press a 3-inch (8 cm) fold over from the top raw edge of the curtain to the wrong side. Pin and baste in place. The top of the curtain will now have a deep pleat in the heading.

10 Cut the heading tape to the width of the curtain plus 1¼ inches (3 cm) at each end. Knot the strings at the leading edge of the curtain and leave them loose at the other end. Place the tape over the raw bottom edge of the fold. Tucking under the ends of the tape, pin, baste, and machine stitch it in place. At the top corners of the curtain, above the gathering tape, slipstitch the folded edges of the toile de Jouy together.

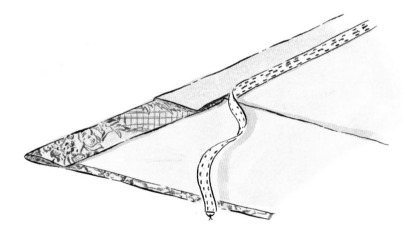

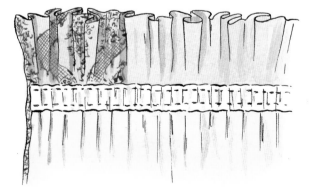

11 Pull the strings of the heading tape into even gathers and knot the ends. Insert the curtain hooks into the gathering tape at regular intervals and hang the curtains from rings threaded on a pole.

equipment and techniques

basic equipment

People planning to make their own curtains will need some basic tools. A pair of good-quality sewing scissors are essential, as are a pair of medium-sized dressmaker's scissors and small embroidery scissors for cutting threads. Equally important are a metal tape measure, yardstick, and a small plastic ruler with which you can measure accurately. Use good-quality steel dressmaker's pins that will not rust, and store them in a box so they stay sharp. A steam iron is invaluable during the finishing process, but should always be used with a damp cloth to protect more delicate fabrics. When marking fabrics, use a vanishing fabric pen, which will fade to invisibility in 72 hours. A metal thimble is another useful item, as is a knitting needle to use to coax ties right side out. Some projects in this book involve making a valance board from plywood. To cut the board to the required shape, you will need a jigsaw, and attaching the valance or curtains to the board may require the use of a staple gun. The projects in this book involve both hand sewing and machine stitches. Basic proficiency in using a sewing machine is necessary, for although it is possible to make curtains entirely by hand, it is a long and laborious job. Your machine should have a good selection of basic stitches. Sophisticated accessories are not needed, but a piping foot is required for some of the projects in this book. Finally, the process of making curtains will be easier and more enjoyable if you work in a well-ventilated and well-lit spot and have access to a large work table.

choosing fabric

For each project the fabrics are specified, since the weight, texture, and pattern is well suited to the particular design. If you want to use an alternative material, select fabric of a similar weight. Always check that your chosen fabric is preshrunk and fade-resistant. Before you cut into the fabric, examine it for any flaws. Minor flaws can sometimes be incorporated into the hem or heading. If the fabric is badly flawed, return it to the retailer or manufacturer. The fire-retardant qualities of upholstery fabrics are governed by legislation in most countries. We suggest that you obtain advice from the manufacturer of your chosen fabric or a specialized upholstery-fabrics retailer, depending on the use you intend for the fabric. Cleaning instructions are printed on the selvages of many fabrics. Any lined or interlined items must always be dry-cleaned.

measuring the window

Before starting to make curtains, you must accurately measure the window to calculate how much fabric you will need. This is a very important calculation, so take your time and carefully check your measurements again once you have finished. If possible, mount the track, pole, or valance board in place before measuring the window. The track or pole should be attached about 2–6 inches (5–15 cm) above the window frame, with the ends projecting at least 4 inches (10 cm) beyond the sides of the window. Take measurements with a steel tape measure for accuracy. If the window is particularly tall or wide, get someone to help you.

2. Divide this measurement by the width of your fabric to calculate how many widths of fabric are required. Round up the final figure to the next full width.
E.g. Width of chosen fabric = 54 inches (135 cm)
Width of fabric needed = 15 feet (4.5 m)
15 feet divided by 54 inches = 3.3
Rounds up to 4

3. Multiply this figure by the unfinished length of the curtain to find out how much fabric is needed.
E.g. Working drop = 10 feet (3 m)
10 x 4 = 40 feet (12 m)
Therefore, the total length of fabric required is 13½ yards (4.2 m), 6¾ yards (2.1 m) for each curtain.

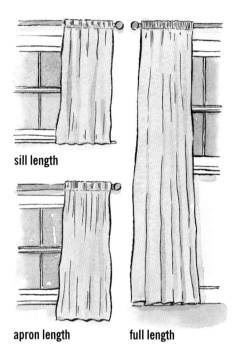

sill length

apron length   **full length**

The two measurements needed in order to calculate fabric quantities for a pair of curtains are the width and the length of the window. To work out the width of the finished curtains, measure the width of the track, rod, or pole (not the window). If you are using a board, measure the sides and front. To calculate the drop of finished full-length drapes, measure from the top of the track or bottom of the pole down to the floor. For sill-length curtains, measure from the top of the track or bottom of the pole down to the sill. For mid-length curtains measure from the top of the track or pole to just below the sill or to the desired point.

calculating fabric quantities
Length
The drop from the pole, track, or rod to the floor, sill, or other desired point determines the length of the finished curtains. Add the appropriate heading and hem allowances (given in the individual projects).

Width
The amount of fabric required is dictated by the curtain heading. Pencil-pleat heading tape, for example, requires fabric that is two and a half times as wide as the pole or track. Add the allowances for hems and joining widths (given in the individual projects).

To calculate how much fabric you will need:

1. Multiply the length of the pole or track by the heading requirement (2½ for pencil-pleat heading) to reach the final fabric width.
E.g. Length of the track or pole = 6 feet (1.8 m)
Pencil-pleat heading = 2½ x length
Width of fabric = 6 x 2½ = 15 feet (4.5 m)

allowing for pattern repeats
If you are using patterned fabric, you will need extra fabric in the length in order to match the pattern across the curtains. To match the pattern, you need to know the length of the pattern repeat (the fabric supplier will be able to provide you with this information). Divide the unfinished length of each curtain by the length of the repeat, round up the result to the next full figure, then multiply it by the length of the repeat to find out how much fabric you will need.
E.g. The unfinished length of your curtain (including allowances) is 4 yards (3.7 m)
144 inches (355 cm)
The pattern repeat is 36 inches (90 cm)
144 divided by 36 = 4
4 multiplied by 36 = 144
Each cut length must be 4 yards (3.7 m) long.

heading requirements

A few standard heading requirements:

gathering tape

2–2½ times length of track

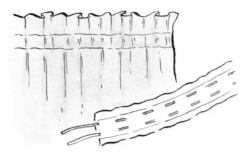

pencil-pleat tape

2½–3 times length of track

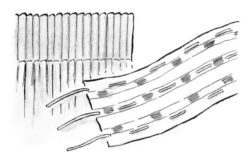

ties

1–2 times length of track

cased heading

2–3 times length of track

cutting out the fabric

It is essential that the fabric is cut straight, or the curtain will hang crooked. Place the fabric on a flat surface. Use a metal ruler and a carpenter's square to mark a straight line in pencil or fabric pen on the wrong side of the fabric. Cut along the line. To cut a width in half, fold it selvage to selvage and cut along the fold. If you are using fabric with a high pile, mark the top of each width with a notch so all the fabric will run in the right direction on the finished curtain.

joining widths

Always place any half widths at the outside edge of the curtain, with a full width at the leading edge. To join two widths, place them right sides together, aligning the raw edges that are to be seamed, and pin, baste, and machine stitch a straight seam ½ inch (1 cm) from the raw edges. Trim away any surplus material. If the fabric puckers, clip the seams so the cloth lies flat.

matching patterns across joined widths

Fold under a ½ inch (1 cm) seam allowance on one width of fabric and press. Lay out the other piece of fabric, right side up, on a flat surface. Place the fabric with the folded edge on the second piece of fabric and match the pattern. Pin in place across the fold.

calculating the size of a valance board

A valance board should be approximately 5–7 inches (12–18 cm) deep, so that the curtains project far enough beyond the window. It must be the width of the window frame plus 4 inches (10 cm) to give clearance at each end.

making a valance board

Cut the plywood to the required proportions and sandpaper any rough edges. Attach a pair of angle brackets to the underneath of the board. This is now the back edge. Two brackets will support a short board; use three or four brackets, evenly spaced, if you have a long or heavy board. If the board is visible behind the curtains, it must be covered. Cut a piece of matching fabric large enough to cover the board, lay it flat, wrong side up, and place the board in the center. Fold the fabric neatly over the board and staple it in place.

basic sewing techniques

basting stitch
This temporary stitch holds fabric in place until it is permanently stitched. Use a contrasting thread so the basting is clearly visible and therefore easy to remove.

slipstitch
Slipstitch holds a folded edge to flat fabric or two folded edges together, as in a mitered corner. Work on the wrong side of the fabric from right to left. Start with the needle in the fold. Push it out and pick up a few threads from the flat fabric, then insert it into the hem again, all in one smooth and continuous movement. When finished, the stitches should be almost invisible.

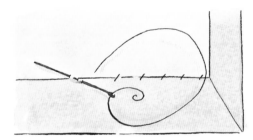

herringbone stitch
This stitch is used to hold a raw edge to flat fabric. Work from left to right with the needle pointing from right to left. Starting in the fold, bring the needle through the hem at a 45° angle. Take a stitch in the single layer of fabric, approximately ¼ inch (5 mm) above the hem, picking up a couple of threads. Bring the needle diagonally down to the hem and make a small backward stitch through one thickness of fabric. Keep the stitches loose.

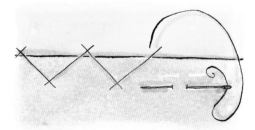

lock stitch
This stitch holds interlining or lining and fabric together. It is a loose stitch, allowing some movement between the layers. It is worked from the bottom of the curtain to the top. Fold back the interlining and make a stitch through the folded interlining and main fabric, picking up only a couple of threads with each stitch. Make the next stitch about 2 inches (5 cm) farther up the interlining. Keep the stitches very slack.

buttonhole stitch
This is used for buttonholes or wherever a raw edge needs to be strengthened or finished neatly. Work from left to right with the raw edge on top. Push the needle through the fabric from back to front, approximately ⅛ inch (2.5 mm) below the raw edge. Twist the thread around the tip of the needle, then pull the needle through to make a knot at the raw edge of the fabric.

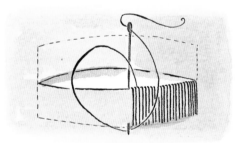

flat seam
This seam is used to join pieces of fabric. Place the two pieces of fabric right sides together, aligning the edges that are to be seamed. Pin and baste, then machine stitch the seam. Reverse the stitches at the beginning and end to secure it in place.

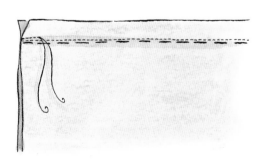

flat fell seam

This sturdy seam is designed for heavy fabric. Pin the fabrics right sides together and baste along the seam line. Machine stitch the seam. Press it open and then over to one side. Trim the underneath seam to half its width. Fold the upper seam allowance over the trimmed one and baste. Machine stitch in place close to the folded edge.

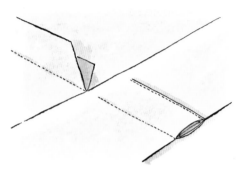

french seam

This self-finishing seam contains all raw edges and is used for sheers and lightweight fabrics. Place two pieces of fabric wrong sides together, aligning the raw edges that are to be seamed. Pin, baste, and machine stitch a seam close to the raw edge. Trim the seam. Fold the material right sides together and pin, baste, and machine stitch a second seam ½ inch (1 cm) from the first, enclosing the raw edges in a narrow tube of fabric.

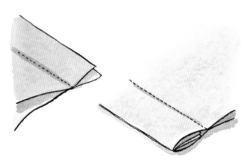

double bottom hem

Most curtains are finished at the bottom with a double hem, which encloses any raw edges and lies flat against the back of the curtain. The bottom hem on lining is also usually finished with a double hem. For a 4-inch (10 cm) double hem, the hem allowance is 8 inches (20 cm). Press up the hem allowance along the bottom edge of the curtain. Open out the hem, then fold the raw edge up to the pressed line. Fold up again and stitch in place.

mitering corners

Mitering is the neatest way of working hem corners. Press in the required hem allowance along the bottom and sides of the fabric, then open them out flat again. Where the two fold lines meet,

make a 45° fold in the fabric and press in place. Turn in the hems along the pressed folds. The edges of the hems will form a neat diagonal line at the corner. Use slipstitch to secure the miter.

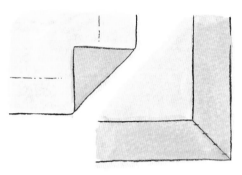

making an angled miter

An angled miter is necessary when a bottom hem is wider than the side hems. Press in the hem allowance along the bottom and sides of the fabric, then open out again. Fold in the corner of the fabric towards the bottom hem of the curtain. Then make the first fold in the double hem. Fold in the side hem, then make the second fold in the double hem. The folded edges should meet.

making ties and tabs

As an alternative to hooks and heading tape, curtains can be attached to a pole or rod with ties. To make a tie, cut a strip of material twice the finished width and length. Fold the strip in half along the length, right sides together. Pin, baste, and machine stitch along the long end and one short end, leaving the other end unstitched. Turn the tie right side out with the aid of a knitting needle. Press a ¼-inch (5 mm) fold to the inside of the tie and slipstitch the end closed. The heavier the curtain, the wider the tie should be. Tabs are made in exactly the same way as ties; but the strip of fabric is wider.

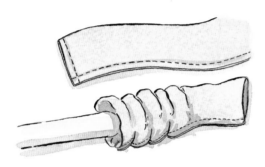

making bias binding

Bias binding is an effective and attractive way to enclose raw edges of fabric. It is available ready made, but it is easy to make. Place your chosen fabric on a flat surface, wrong side up. Diagonally fold in one corner until the end of the fabric is aligned with the selvage, forming a triangle of fabric. The diagonal fold line is the bias line of the material. Mark strips parallel to the bias line all the way across the fabric and cut them out.

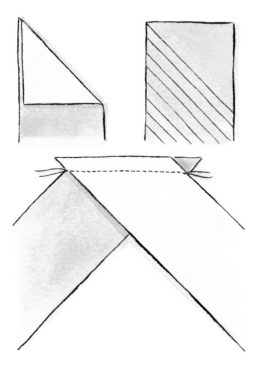

Join the strips to make a continuous strip of bias binding. Place two strips right sides together at right angles, lining up the raw edges. Pin and machine stitch together, using a ⅜-inch (7 mm) seam allowance. Trim the seams, press flat, and trim the corners.

making corded piping

Piping is made from a length of cord covered with bias binding. The binding must be wide enough to cover the cord and to allow a ⅝-inch (1.5 cm) seam allowance on each side of it. Wrap the binding around the cord, then baste and machine stitch close to the cord, using a piping foot.

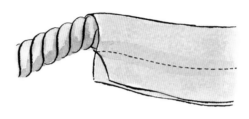

making box pleats

Box pleats give a tailored finish to curtains and valances. One box pleat uses fabric three times the width of the pleat. Decide on the finished width of each pleat and multiply it by three. The finished width of the object you are making must be divisible by this measurement. For example, if each pleat is 4 inches (10 cm) wide, the width of the item to be pleated must be exactly divisible by 12 inches (30 cm). If it is not, adjust either the width of the object or the width of the pleat. For a 4-inch (10 cm) pleat, mark a fold 2 inches from the edge of the fabric and another 2 inches (5 cm) from that. Then mark alternate 4-inch (10 cm) and 2-inch (5 cm) folds across the top of the fabric. Fold along the first mark, 2 inches (5 cm) from the edge of the curtain, and bring it across to join a mark 8 inches (20 cm) on from it. Pin the folds together. Leave a 4-inch (10 cm) space and repeat the action all the way across the width of the fabric to form the rest of the pleats.

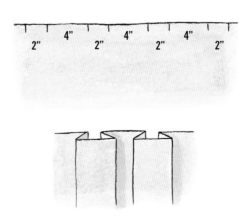

templates

All the templates in this book must be enlarged.
Either use a photocopier to enlarge the template to the desired
proportions (sometimes stated in the individual project) on heavy
paper or cardboard, or trace the pattern onto graph paper,
increase the proportions to the desired size, then transfer to heavy
paper or cardboard. Cut out the template. Pin it to the wrong side
of your fabric, then mark all the way around the outline of the
template in fabric pen.

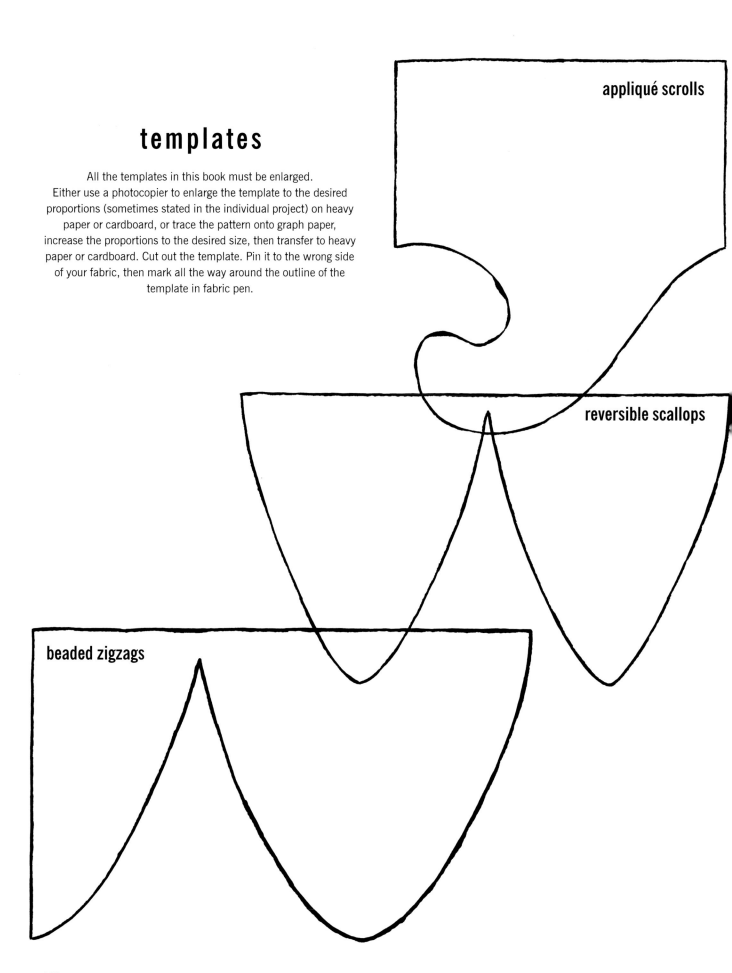

appliqué scrolls

reversible scallops

beaded zigzags

Nicole Fabre Textiles
www.nicolefabredesigns.com

Nordic Style
www.nordicstyle.com

Osborne & Little
979 Third Avenue
New York NY 10022
Tel: 212 751 3333
www.osborneandlittle.com

Ralph Lauren Home
867 Madison Avenue
New York NY 10021
Tel: 888 475 7674
www.rlhome.polo.com

Rogers & Goffigon Ltd.
979 Third Avenue
New York NY 10022
Tel: 212 888 3242

Sanderson
979 Third Avenue
New York NY 10022
Tel: 212 319 7220
www.sanderson-online.co.uk

Scalamandre Fabrics
222 East 59th Street
New York NY 10022
Tel: 212 980 3888
www.scalamandre.com

Schumacher & Co.
979 Third Avenue
New York NY 10022
Tel: 800 332 3384
www.fschumacher.com

Travers Fabrics
979 Third Avenue
New York NY 10022
Tel: 212 888 7900
www.traversinc.com

V.V. Rouleaux
www.vvrouleaux.com

Waverly Fabrics
www.waverly.com

Westgate Fabrics
905 Avenue T Suite 905
Grand Prairie TX 75053
Tel: 800 527 2517
www.westgatefabrics.com

Zoffany
979 Third Avenue
New York NY 10022
Tel: 212 593 9787
www.zoffany.uk.com

Ready- and custom-made curtain suppliers

Bed, Bath, & Beyond
620 Avenue of the Americas
New York NY 10011
Tel: 212 255 3550
www.bedbathandbeyond.com

Castle Draperies
23287 Ventura Boulevard
Woodland Hills
CA 91364
Tel: 818 883 7273
www.castledraperies.com

Country Curtains
Tel: 800 456 0321
www.countrycurtains.com

Gracious Home
1220 Third Avenue
New York NY 10021
Tel: 212 517 6300
www.gracioushome.com

Jo-Ann
13323 Riverside Drive
Sherman Oaks
CA 91423-2508
Tel: 818-789-3167
Tel: 1-800-525-4951 for enquiries
www.joann.com

Lowe's
5200 Franklin Street
Michigan City
IN 46360
Tel: 219 872 2900
www.lowes.com

Michaels
Tel: 1-800-MICHAELS for a store near you
www.michaels.com

Pier One Imports
71 Fifth Avenue
New York NY 10003
Tel: 212 206 1911
www.pier1.com

Pottery Barn
600 Broadway
New York NY 10012
Tel: 800 922 5507
www.potterybarn.com

Sunshine Drapery Company
11660 Page Service Drive
St. Louis MO 63146
Tel: 314 569 2980
www.sunshinedrapery.com

credits

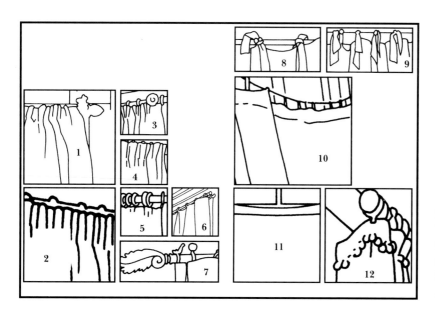

page 1   antique fabric
page 2   fabrics from Sanderson, pole from Byron & Byron
page 4   above from left to right: plain fabric from Sanderson, checked fabric from KA International; fabric from Sanderson, tension wire kit from Ikea; below: fabric from Streets
page 5   from left to right: both fabrics from KA International; antique fabric
page 7   ready-made curtains from Habitat

use of fabrics *pages 8–9*
1   antique curtains
2   fabric, fringe and pole from John Lewis
3   antique fabric
4   ready-made curtains from Habitat
5   fabric from Osborne & Little, pole and brackets from Byron & Byron
6   Toile de Jouy from Christopher Moore Textiles, pole from McKinney & Co
7   ready-made curtains from Habitat

projects: yellow checks: fabrics from Ian Mankin, trimmings from V. V. Rouleaux • horizontal stripes: fabrics from Sanderson, poles, brackets and rings from Byron & Byron • two-way striped voile: antique fabric • appliqué scrolls: fabrics from Sanderson, pole and brackets from Byron & Byron • contrast-bordered linen: linen from Nicole Fabre, curtains by Reed Creative Services

headings *pages 30–31*
1   antique voile and fixtures
2   fabric from Streets, pole from Hallis Hudson
3   antique linen, pole and brackets from McKinney & Co
4   fabric from Jane Churchill, pole from McKinney & Co
5   fabric from Ian Mankin, pole and rings from John Lewis
6   vintage fabric, poles from Hallis Hudson, antique ring clips from McKinney & Co
7   fabric from Habitat, pole from McKinney & Co
8   fabric from Shaker, pole from Bradley
9   fabric from Sanderson, pole from Byron & Byron
10   fabric from Ian Mankin
11   fabric from Nordic Style
12   fabric, pole and fringe from John Lewis fabric from Ian Mankin

projects: reversible scallops: fabric from Pierre Frey • button-on silk: fabric from Pongees, ammonite knobs from John Lewis • concertina stripes: fabric from Sanderson, tension wire kit from Ikea • tie-on muslin sheers: muslin from JAB, pole made to order

projects: gathered gingham: fabric from John Lewis • monogrammed linen valance: fabric from Streets • beaded zigzags: fabric from Ian Sanderson, beads from John Lewis • red-trimmed voile: fabric from Sanderson, binding from John Lewis • shaped linen valance: fabric from Sahco Hesslein • rope-edged valance: fabric from Designers Guild, rope trim from V. V. Rouleaux • gypsy-skirted valance: vintage fabric, glass beads from V. V. Rouleaux

projects: Italian stringing with bow: fabric from Jane Churchill • squares on squares: plain fabric from Sanderson, checked fabric from KA International • contrast-scalloped border: fabric from Streets, felt from B. Brown, pole from Hallis Hudson • pictorial-edged curtains: both fabrics from KA International

glossary

Appliqué
Applying a second layer of fabric to a main fabric, usually with decorative stitching.

Bias binding
A strip of cloth cut on the bias, at 45° to the selvage, which gives stretch to the fabric. Used as edging or to cover piping cord.

Box pleat
A flat symmetrical pleat formed by folding the fabric to the back at each side of the pleat.

Braid
A woven ribbon used as edging or trimming.

Buckram
Burlap, or another coarse cloth, stiffened with size and used to give rigidity to valances.

Burlap
A strong, coarse fabric made from jute or hemp fibers.

Cased heading
A simple curtain heading in which a sleeve of material is left open at the top of the curtain to receive a curtain rod or pole.

Corded piping
A length of cord covered with bias binding, used as a decorative edging.

Cotton
A natural fabric, made from the boll of the cotton plant.

Eyelet
A metal ring punched through fabric to create a bound hole through which poles, rods, or wire can be inserted.

Felt
Unwoven cloth made from pounded wool. The edges do not fray after cutting.

Finial
A decorative fixture attached to each end of a curtain pole to hold the curtains on the pole.

Gathering tape
A heading tape that creates an informal shallow, ruffled effect.

Gingham
A plain weave cotton cloth with a checked pattern.

Heading
The top of a curtain, finished with tape, ties, rings, or other treatments.

Heading tape
Ready-made tape that is attached to the top of a curtain to create a particular heading.

Interlining
A soft material inserted between fabric and lining that provides insulation and gives the curtains a luxurious padded quality.

Italian stringing
A method of opening curtains with a heading that is kept permanently closed. Cord is threaded through rings on the back of the curtain, then pulled to draw the leading edges apart.

Laminate
A thin protective covering, bonded to a material.

Leading edge
The inside edges of a pair of curtains.

Lining fabric
A secondary fabric used to back curtains and protect them from light and dust. Usually cotton sateen fabric with a slight sheen.

Miter
A diagonal seam between two pieces of fabric formed at a corner.

Pencil pleat heading
A popular heading tape that creates regular, stiff pleats.

Pleat
A fold or crease, pressed or stitched in place.

Raw edge
The cut edge of fabric, without selvage or hem.

Seam allowance
The narrow strip of raw-edged fabric left on each side of a stitched seam.

Selvage
Defined warp edge of the fabric, woven to prevent unraveling.

Sheers
Fine, translucent fabrics such as voile that filter daylight while preserving daytime privacy.

Silk
A luxurious and soft yet strong fabric produced by silkworms.

Ticking
A striped, closely woven heavy cotton twill fabric.

Toile de Jouy
A cotton cloth printed with pastoral scenes in a single color on a neutral background.

Valance
A strip of fabric that runs across the top of a window. It can be glued, nailed, or hung from a mounting board positioned above the window frame.

Voile
A light plain-weave cotton or man-made fabric.

Width
The distance from selvage to selvage on any fabric.

index

acknowledgments

Many thanks to all the fabric companies and their public relations staff who so generously gave us yards and yards of fabric to make up the curtains for this book. They include Jane Churchill, Designers Guild, Pierre Frey, KA International, Ian Mankin, Osborne & Little, Sahco Hesslein, Sanderson, and Shaker. Thanks also to Tim Leese and Bobby Chance, Liz Shirley, Susie Tinsley, and Fiona Wheeler for kindly allowing us to invade their houses and festoon every window with curtains to photograph. Hänsi Schneider has made most of the curtains in this book with her usual superb skill and talent. Many thanks always. Helena Lynch also made some of the curtains—brilliantly. James Merrell has taken superb photographs of a difficult subject with his usual calm control. Thank you to Michael Hill for his wonderful illustrations and to all at Ryland Peters & Small for another good team effort. Finally, many thanks to Catherine Coombes, for her huge hard work, both on this book, and at home.

dedication

For Janey Joicey-Cecil, a true and loving friend, with gratitude